FAMILY ALBUM
January 2013

Artist's Statement:

The following photographs form a family album—not of the persons in my family, but of the businesses once owned. When my father's family immigrated to this country, most branches of the family started their own grocery stores; after 70 years, the last of them are closing. These businesses, as are most small businesses, were the locus of each family. I documented the state of each business's building over the month of January 2013--whether it was last owned by someone in the family 50 years ago or yesterday. Each photograph is titled by its place in the sequence of photographs, the name of the business depicted, address of the business, and the dates the business was run by my relatives, as best approximated; these titles should be considered to be part of the artwork. Furthermore, the photographs are ordered in such a way that reflect their ownership, primarily by familial branch.

It should be noted here that this is not a comprehensive album. The project was limited to the stores of my paternal grandparents, their siblings, and first cousins, as best could be ascertained in January. Even within this limited range, however, certain stores were omitted: among other reasons, some relatives could not be contacted, other relatives had fallen out of touch, and some businesses had simply been forgotten. Many of the dates listed are, at best, approximations, and all stores were located in California's Central Valley, where most of my relatives settled. While the photographs mean to tell the story of my family, and, to an extent, that of their domicile, the project as a whole also reflects on questions relating to history, its methods, and its epistemological concerns. Because of this, I chose only to use photographs from the current day, and to present stores still under family ownership through January 31st, 2013 as extant in the body of the project. Those that have closed since January are instead noted in the Appendix.

Finally, I would like to thank my family—it would have been impossible to put this project together without their support, and for that I am eternally grateful.

Bryan Chong
September 1, 2013
Brooklyn, NY

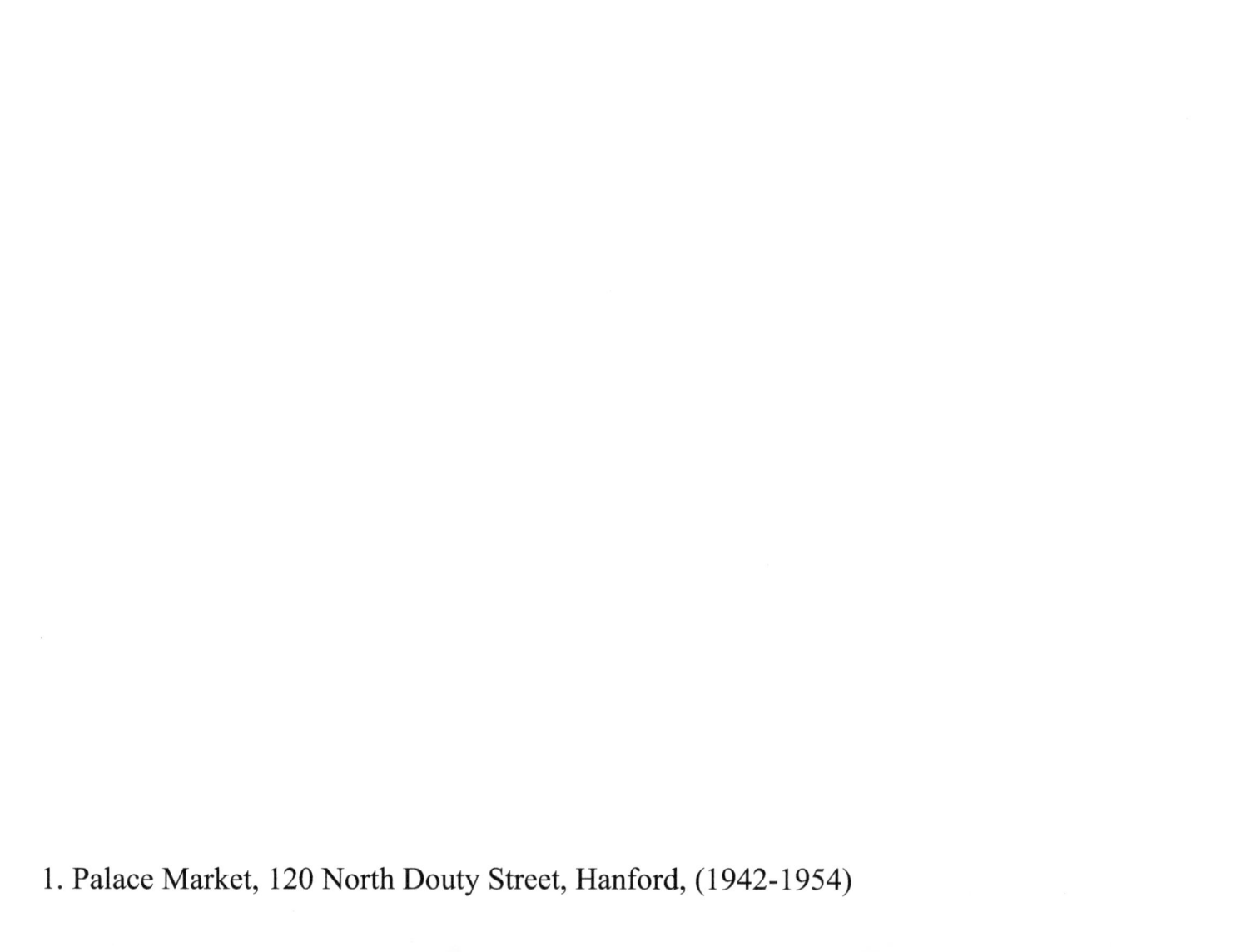

1. Palace Market, 120 North Douty Street, Hanford, (1942-1954)

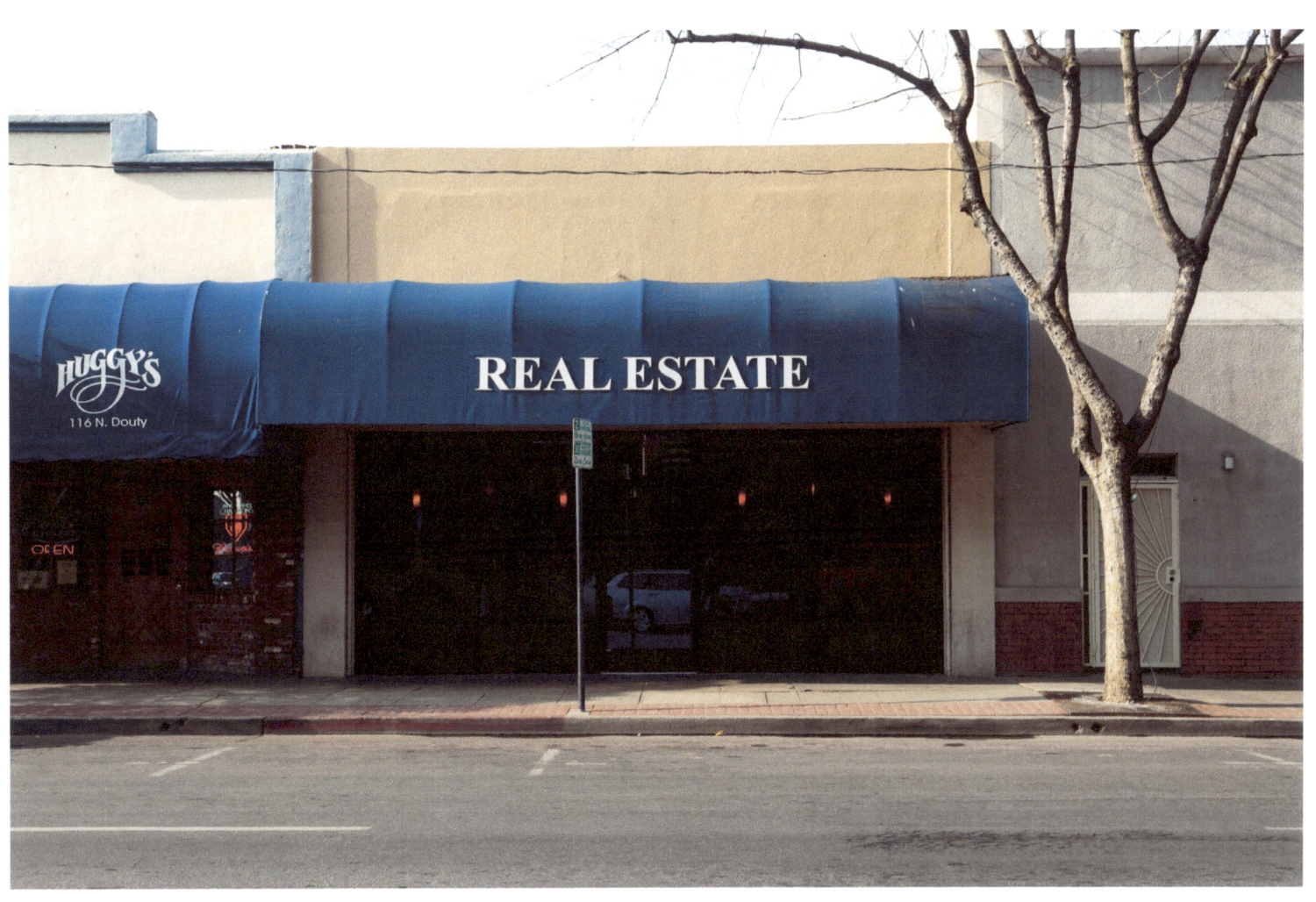

2. Sequoia Super Market, 2000 North Central Avenue, Ceres (1955-2005)

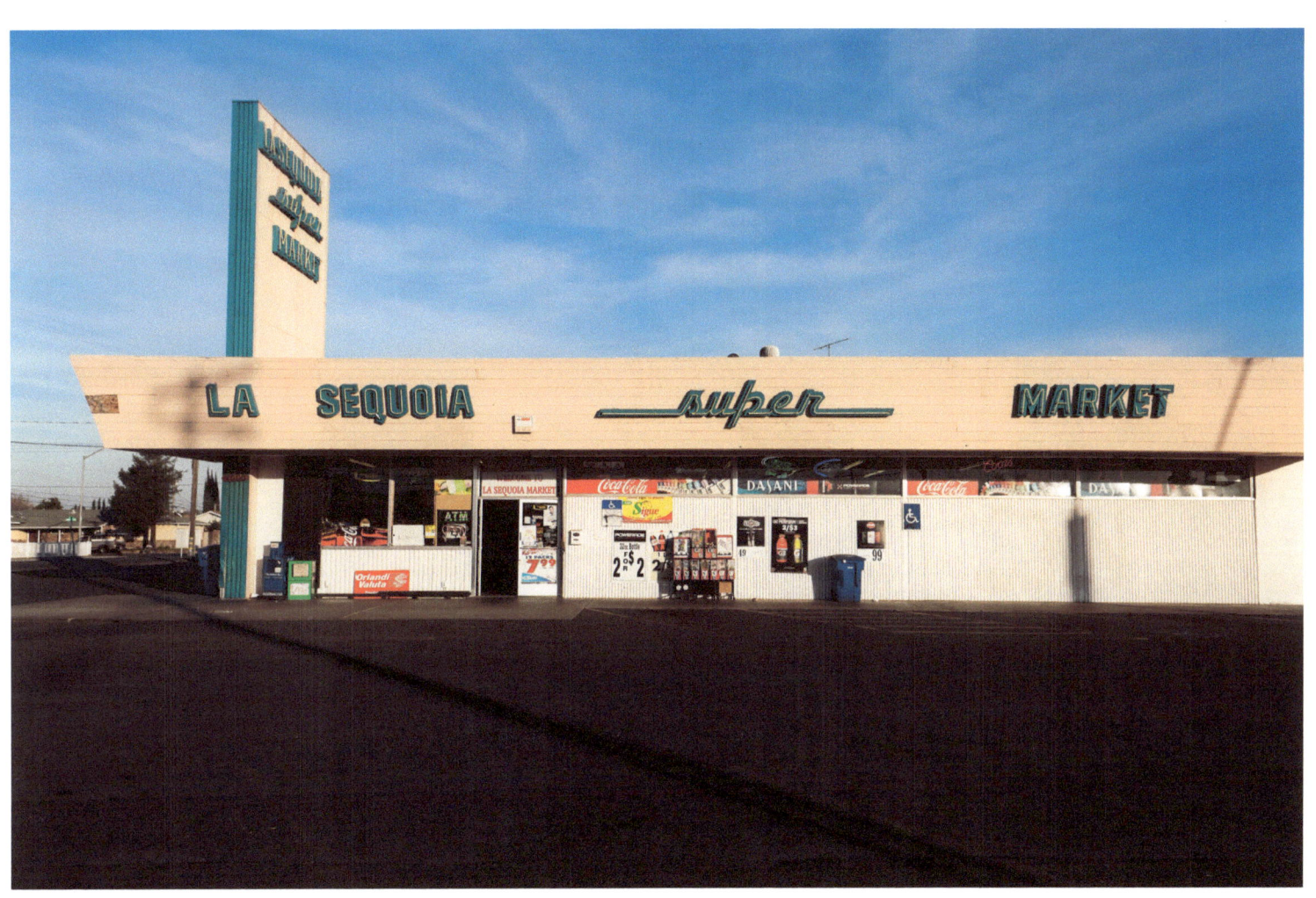

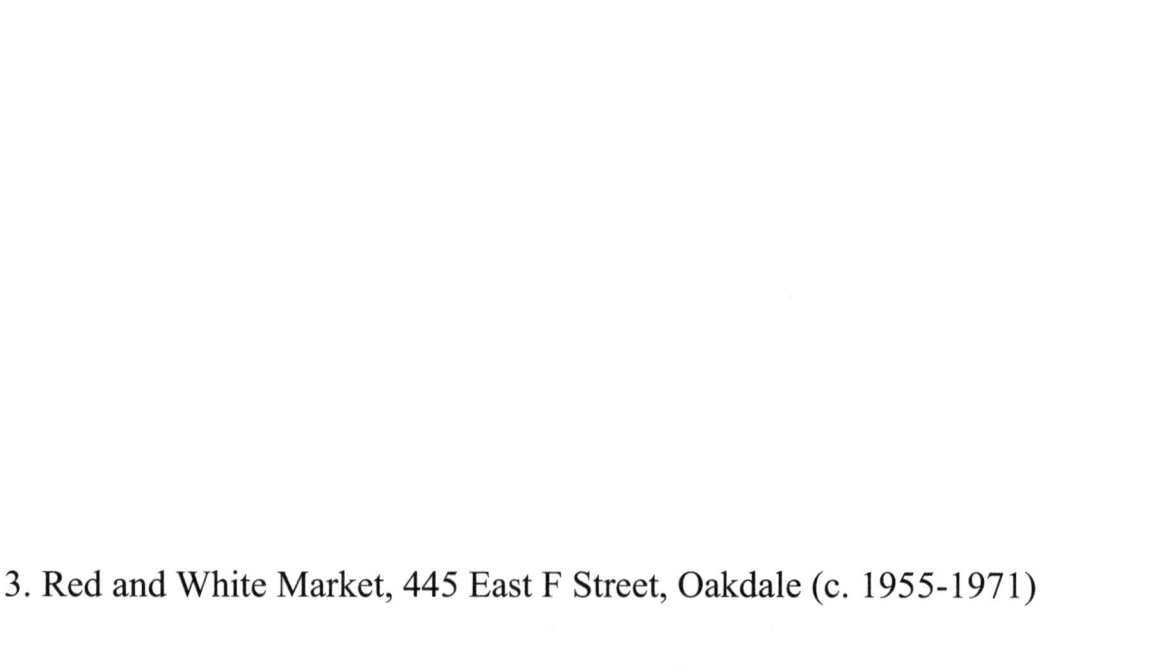

3. Red and White Market, 445 East F Street, Oakdale (c. 1955-1971)

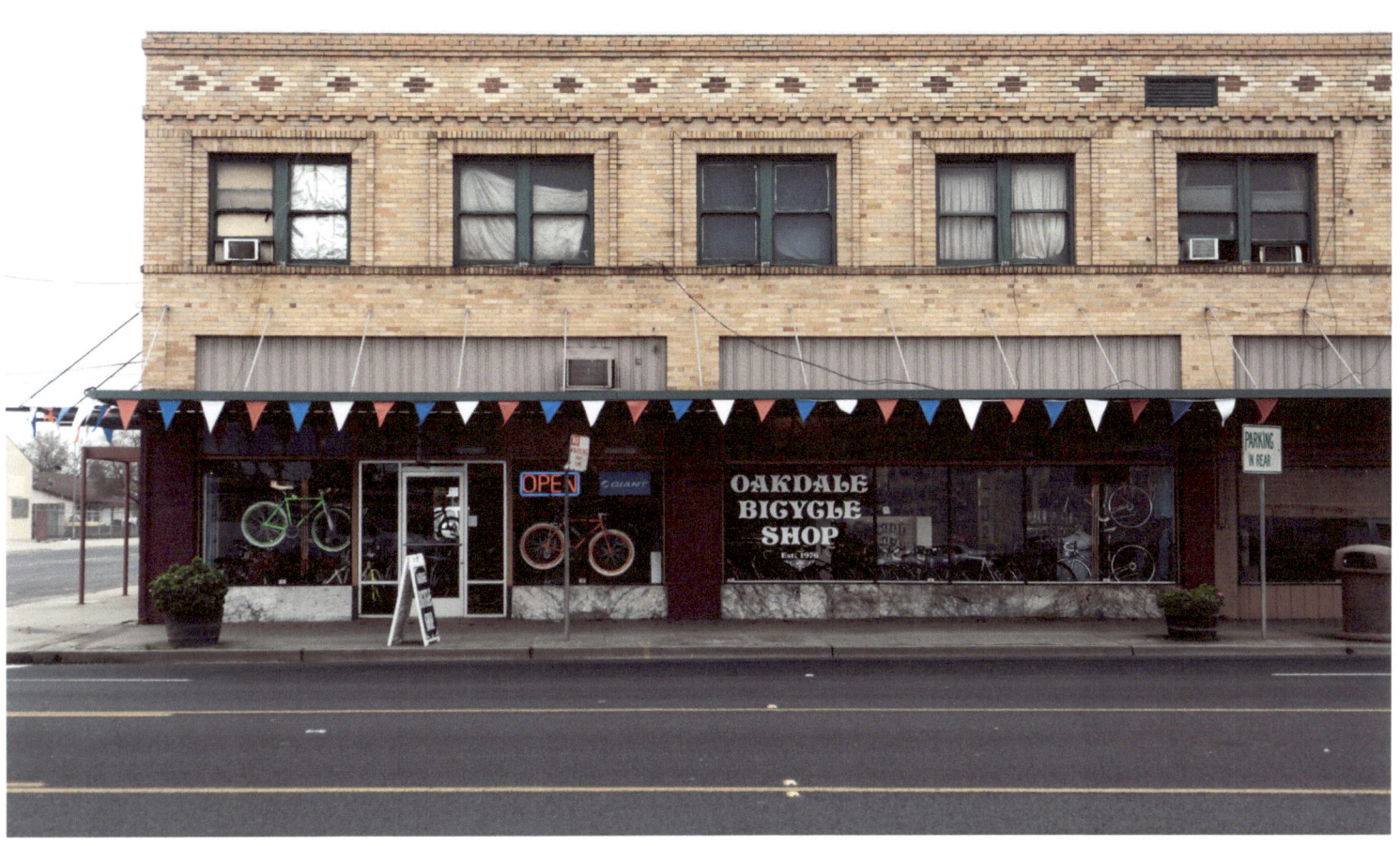

4. Monte Food Market, 2202 East Fremont Street, Stockton (c. 1972-1985)

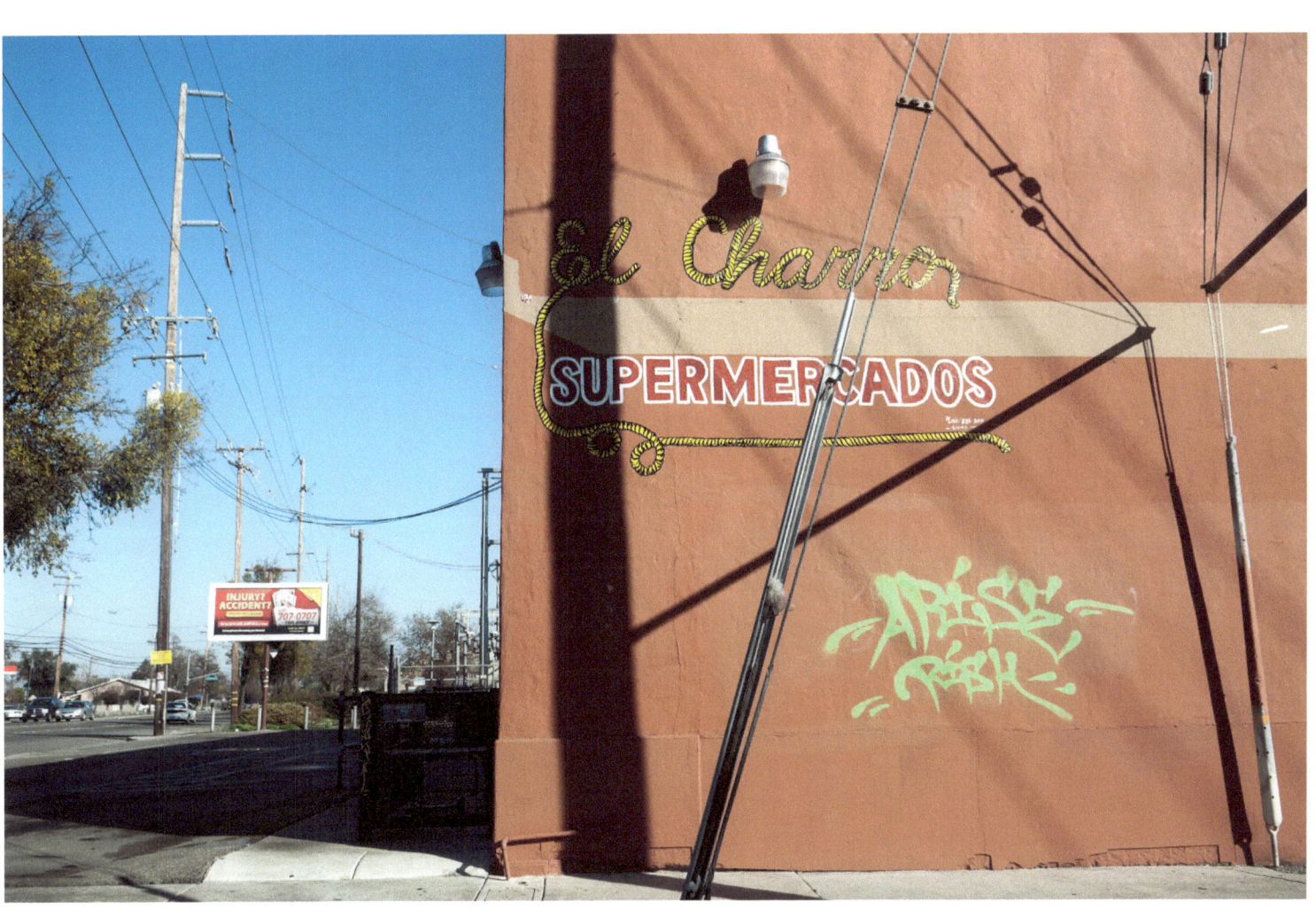

5. Sam's Food City I, 1046 Fresno Street, Newman, (1954-1988)

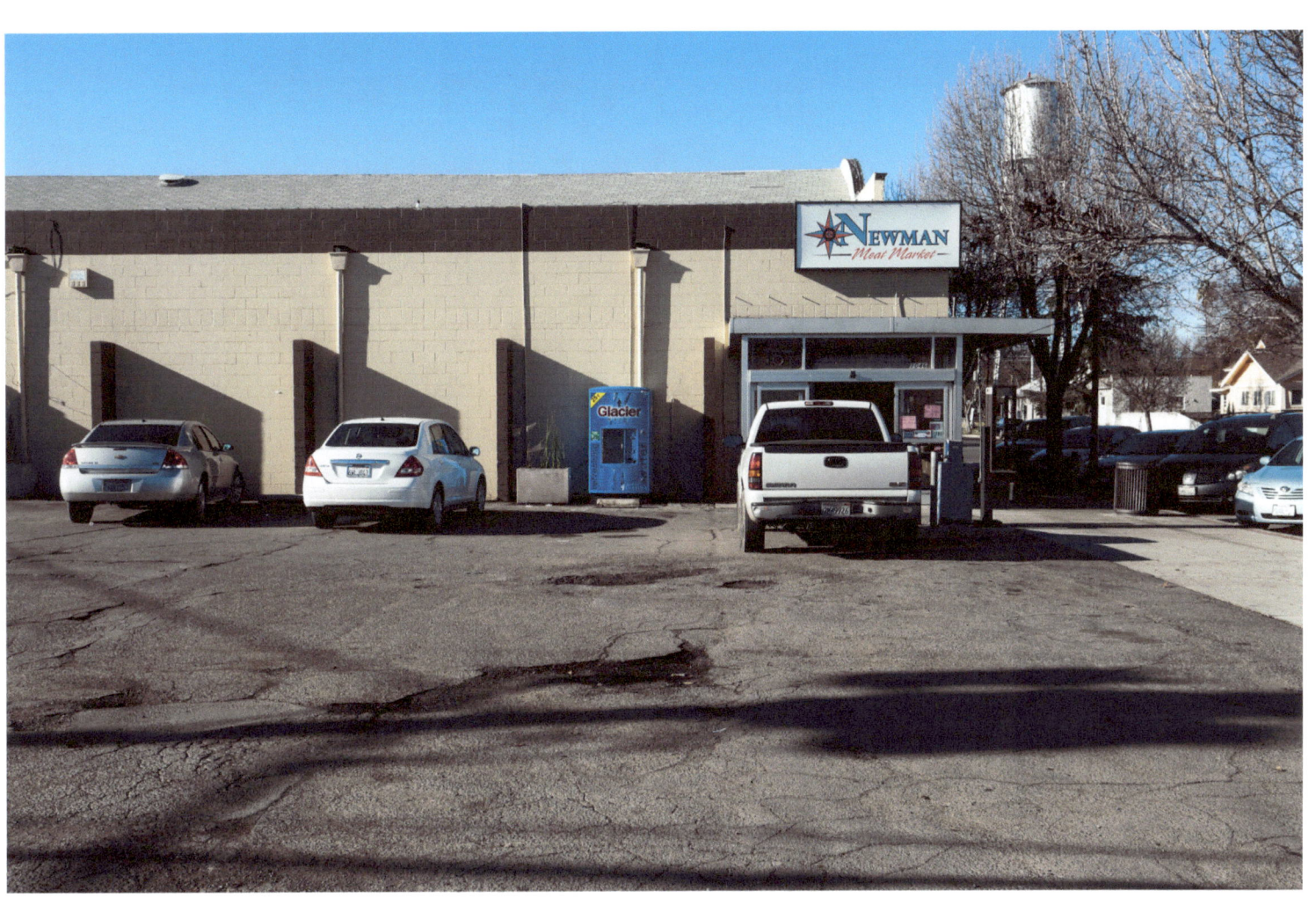

6. Sam's Food City II, 1100 Carver Road, Modesto (1962-)

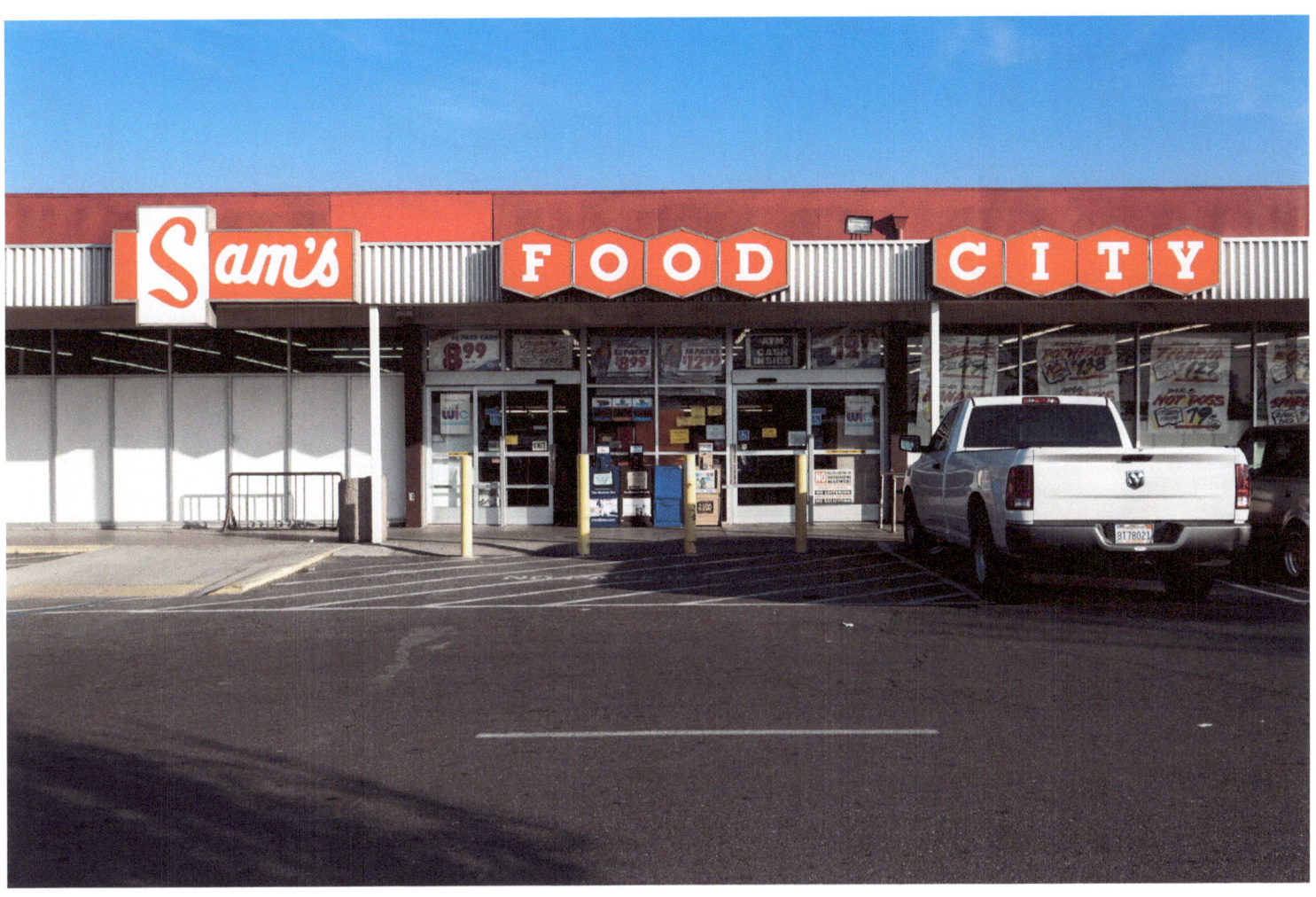

7. Sam's Food City III, 323 Cressey Road, Livingston (1981-)

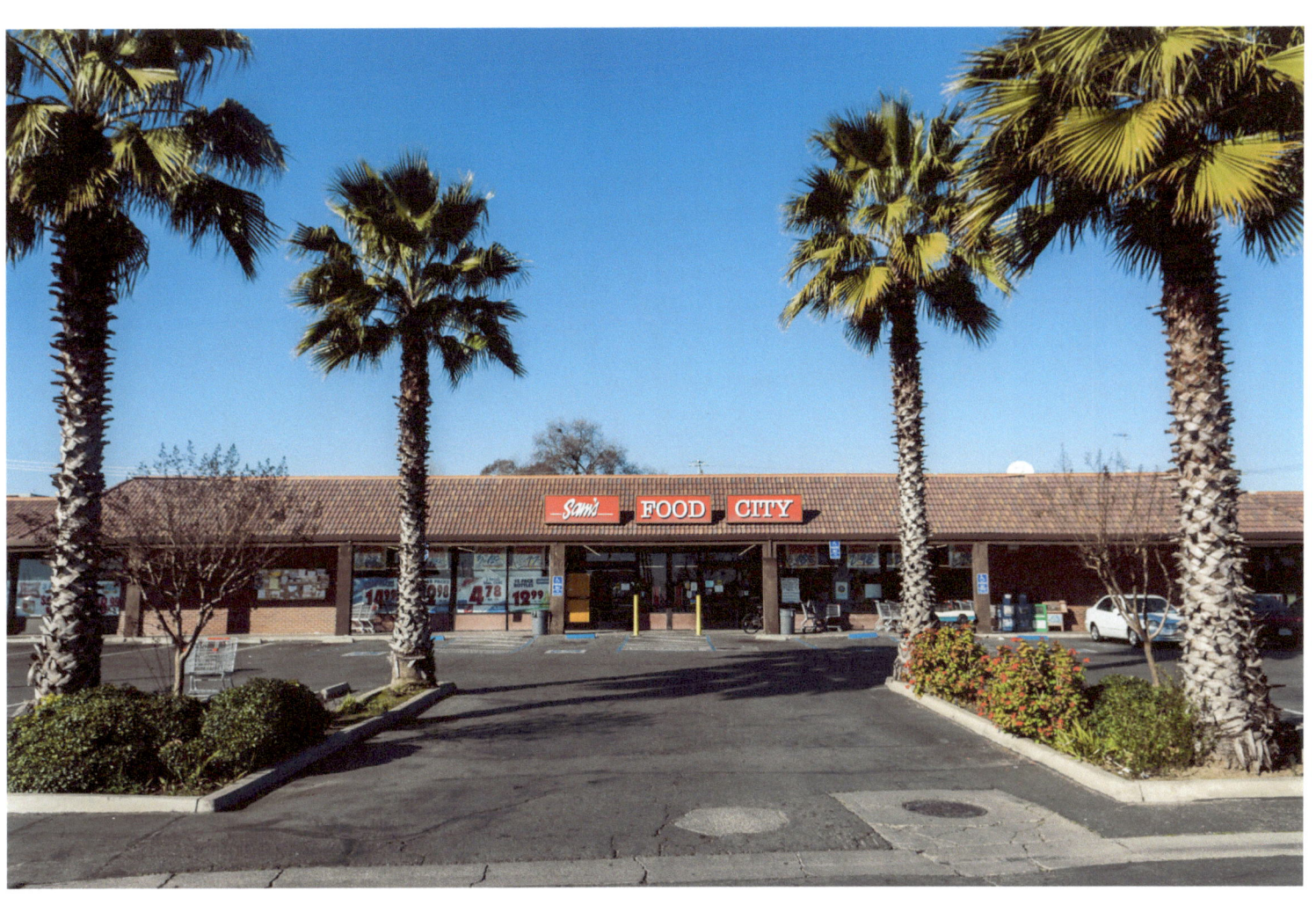

8. Sam's Food City IV, 125 South Circulo Avenue, Patterson (1985-2012)

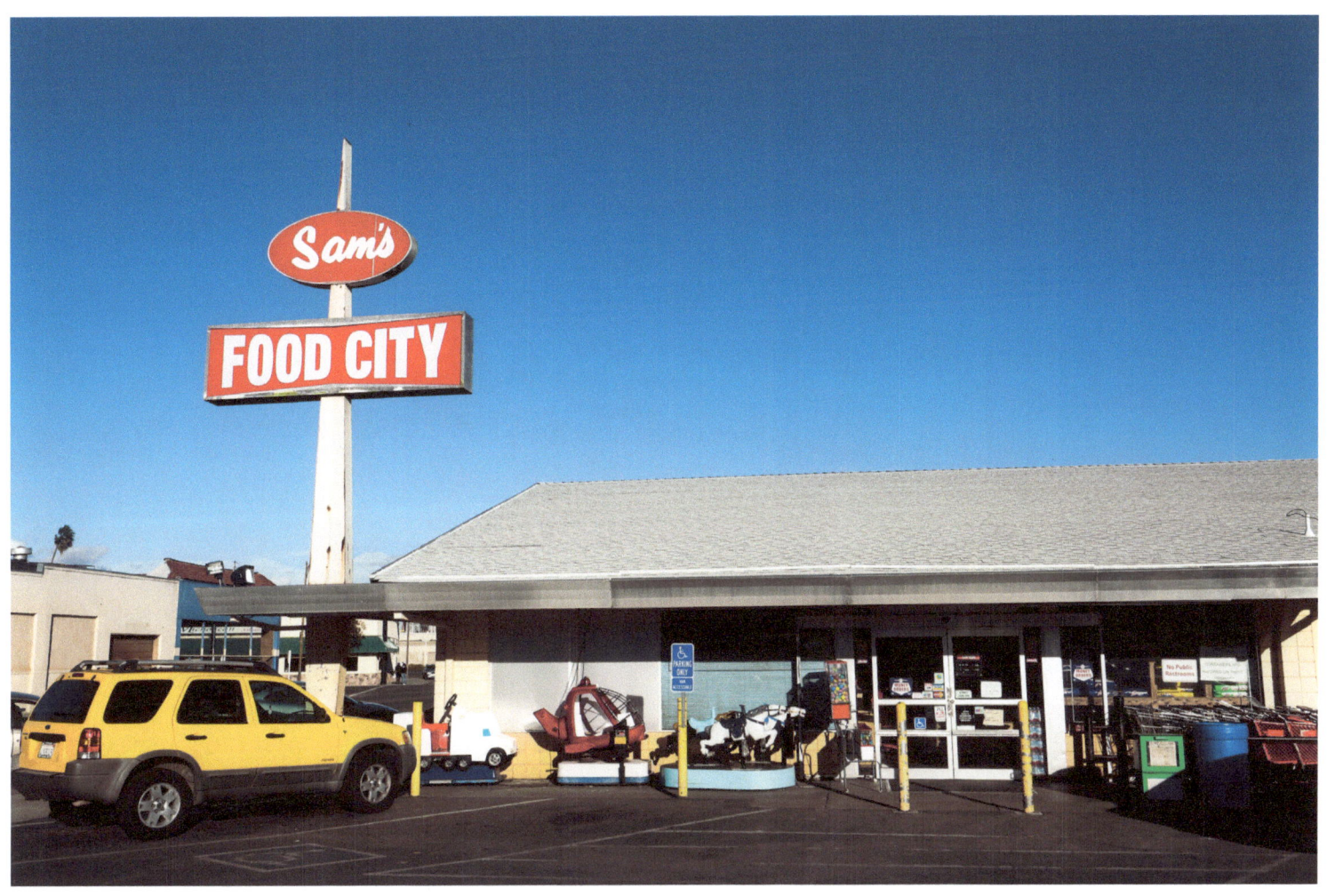

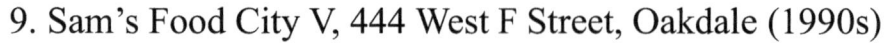

9. Sam's Food City V, 444 West F Street, Oakdale (1990s)

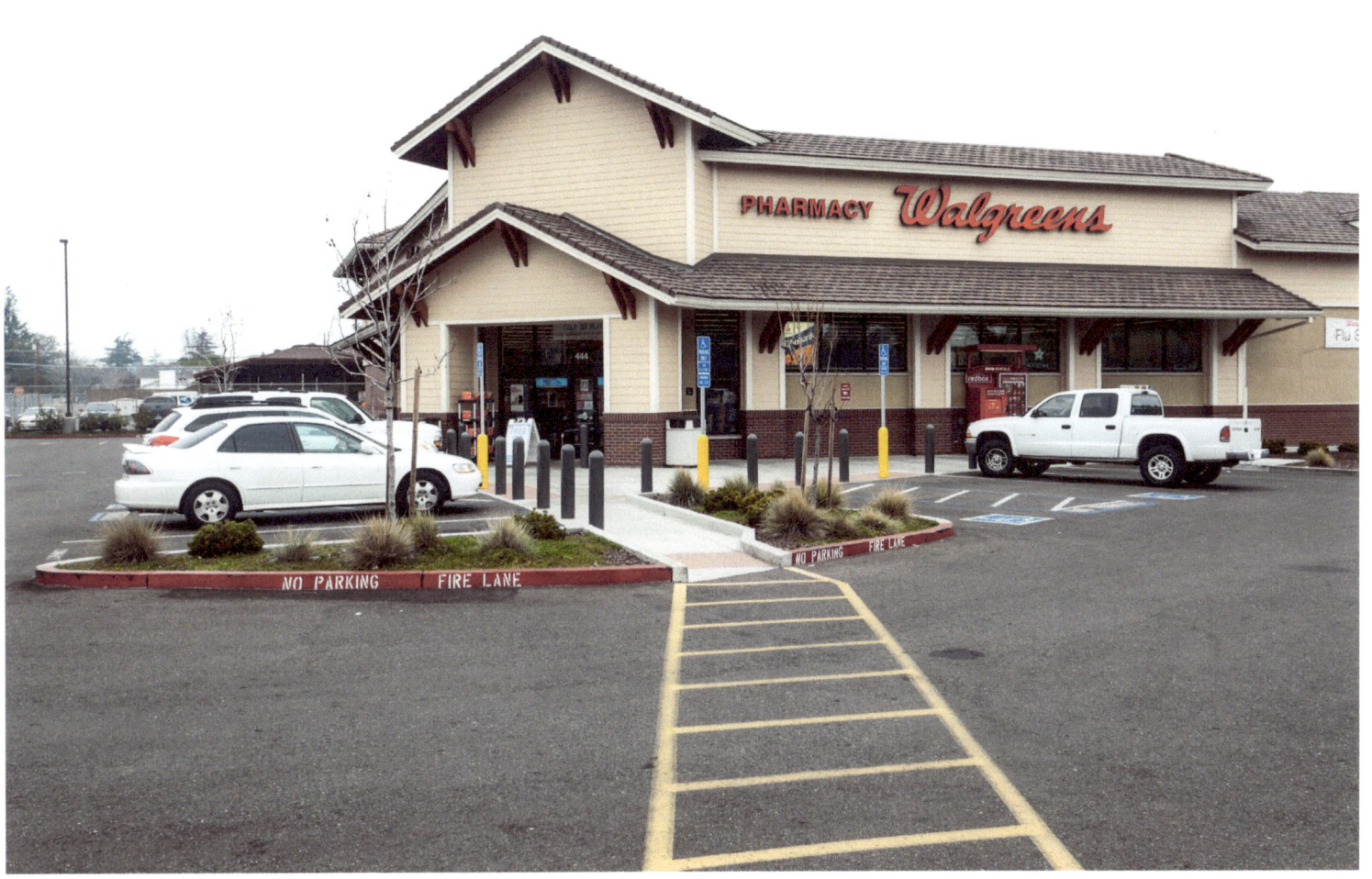

10. Sam's Food City VI, 965 Lander Avenue, Turlock (1997-)

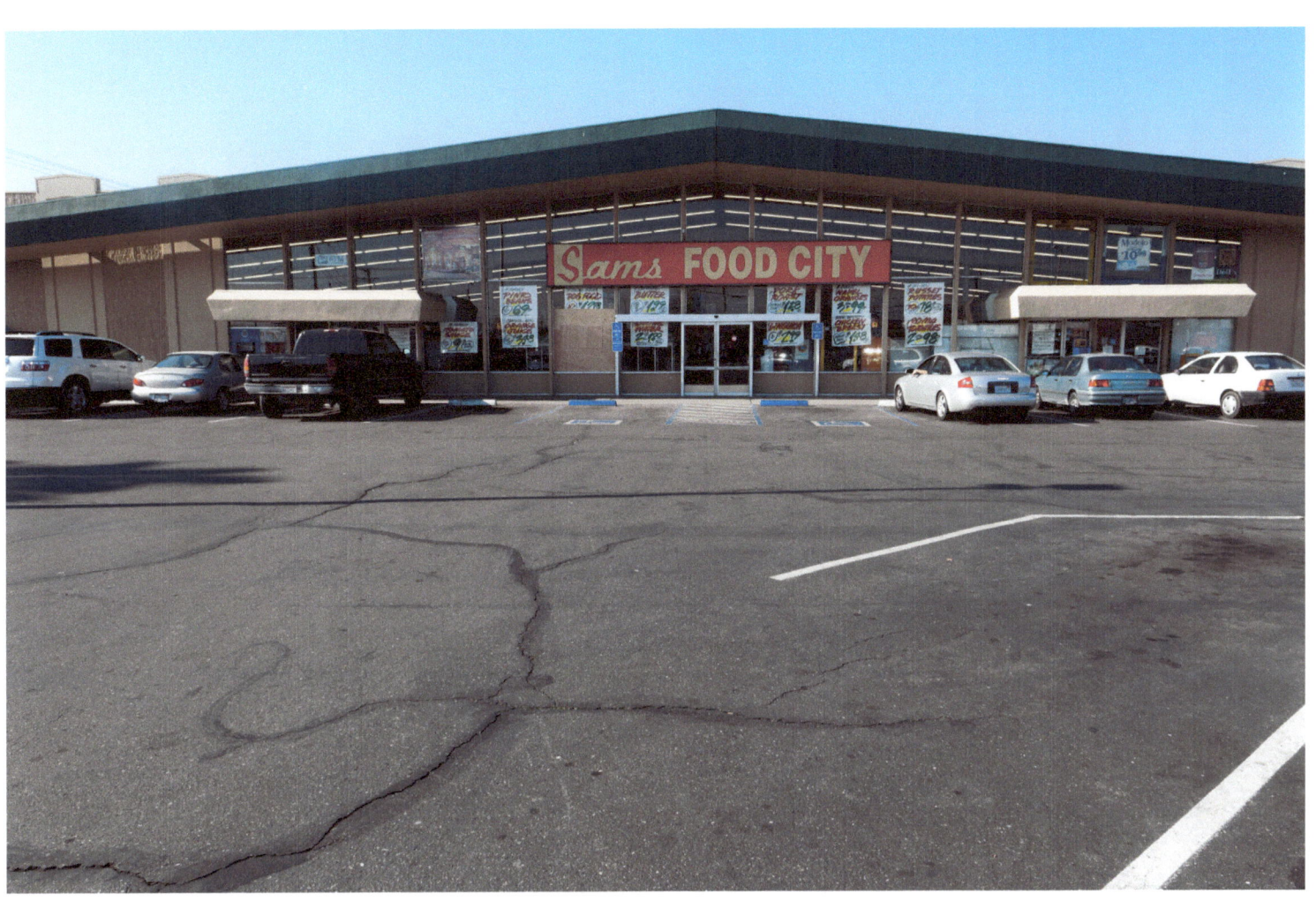

11. National Market, 1290 East Avenue, Turlock (1951-)

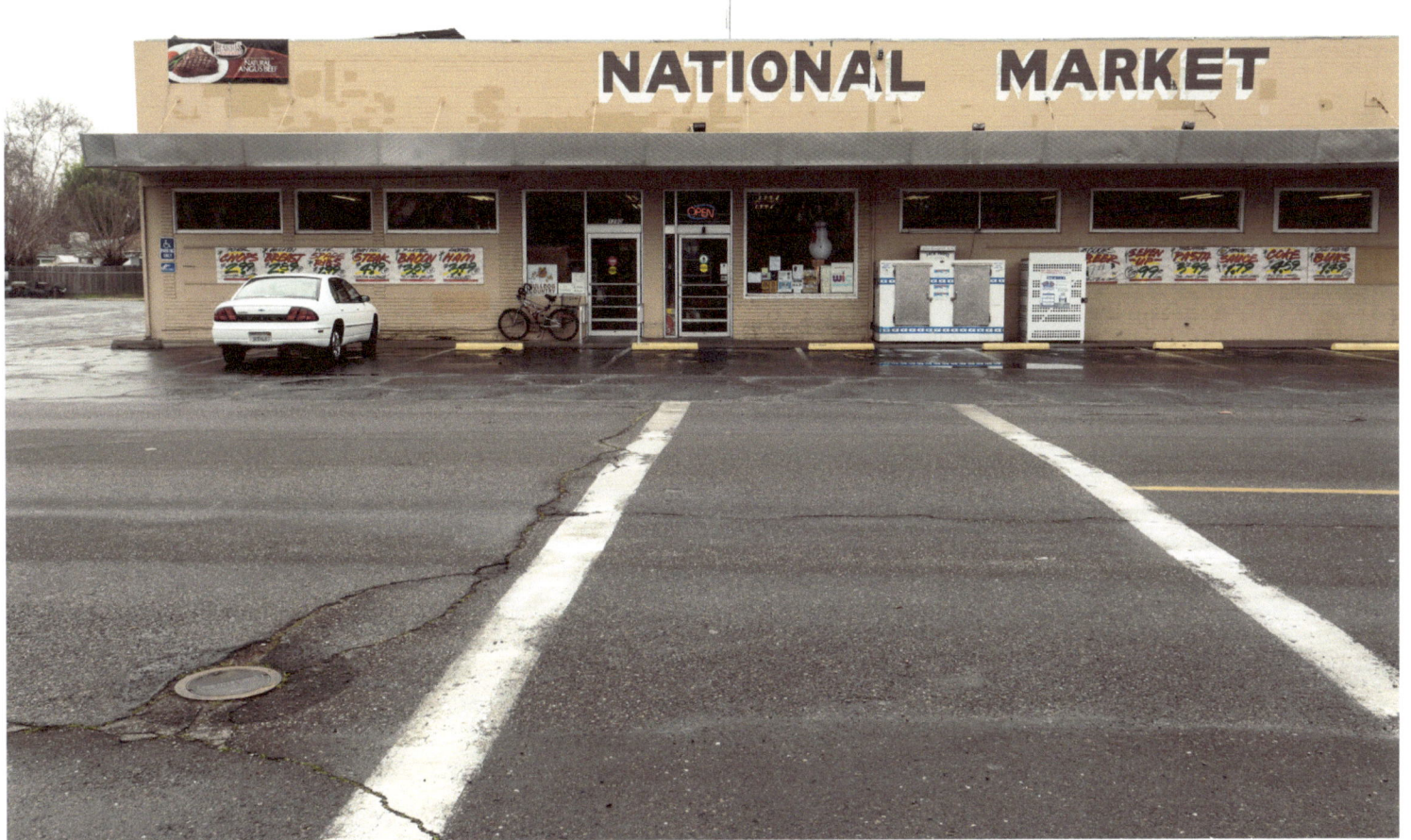

12. Livingston Food Center, 334 Main Street, Livingston (mid-1950s-1963)

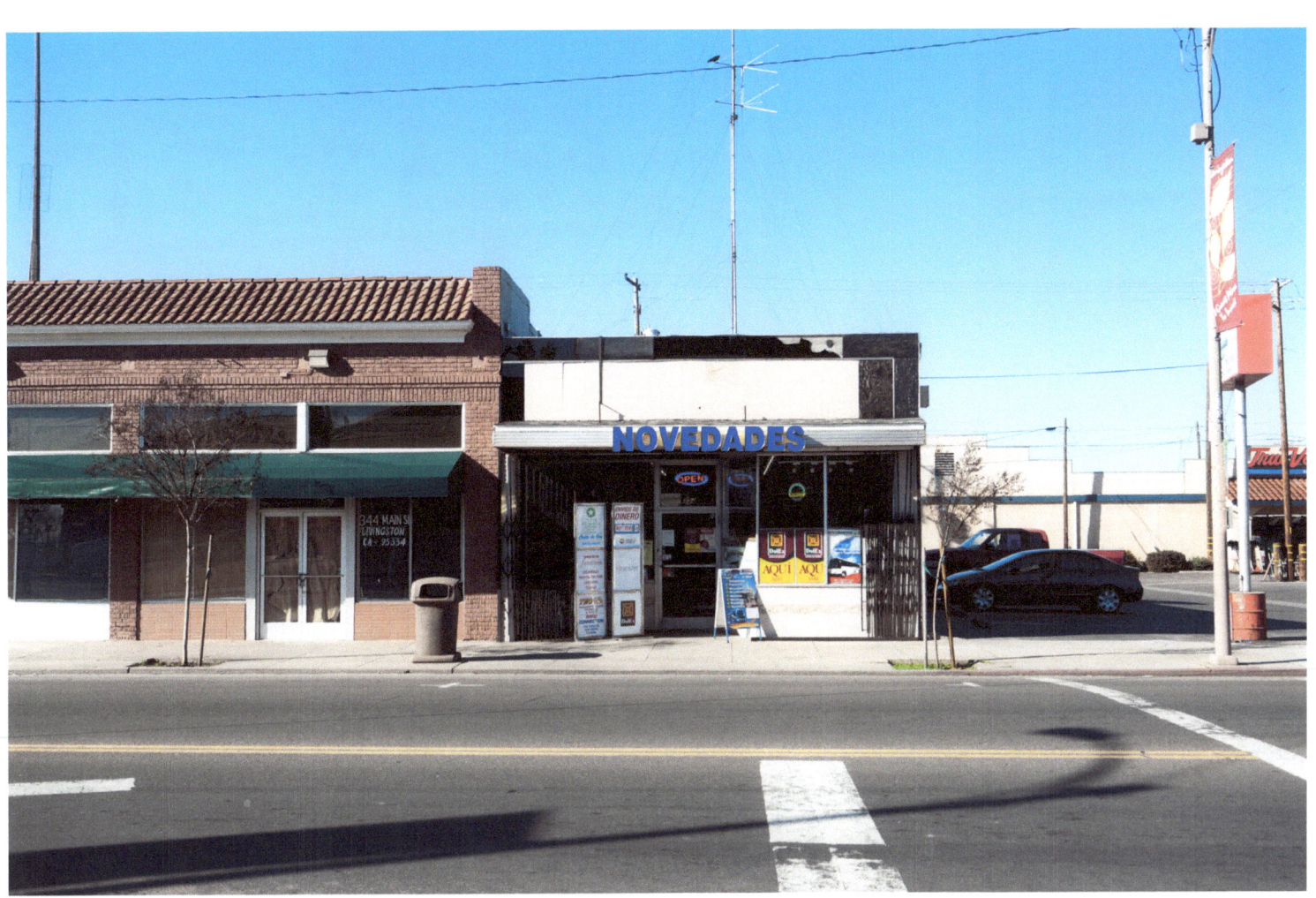

13. Value Market, 1724 Main Street, Livingston, (1963-)

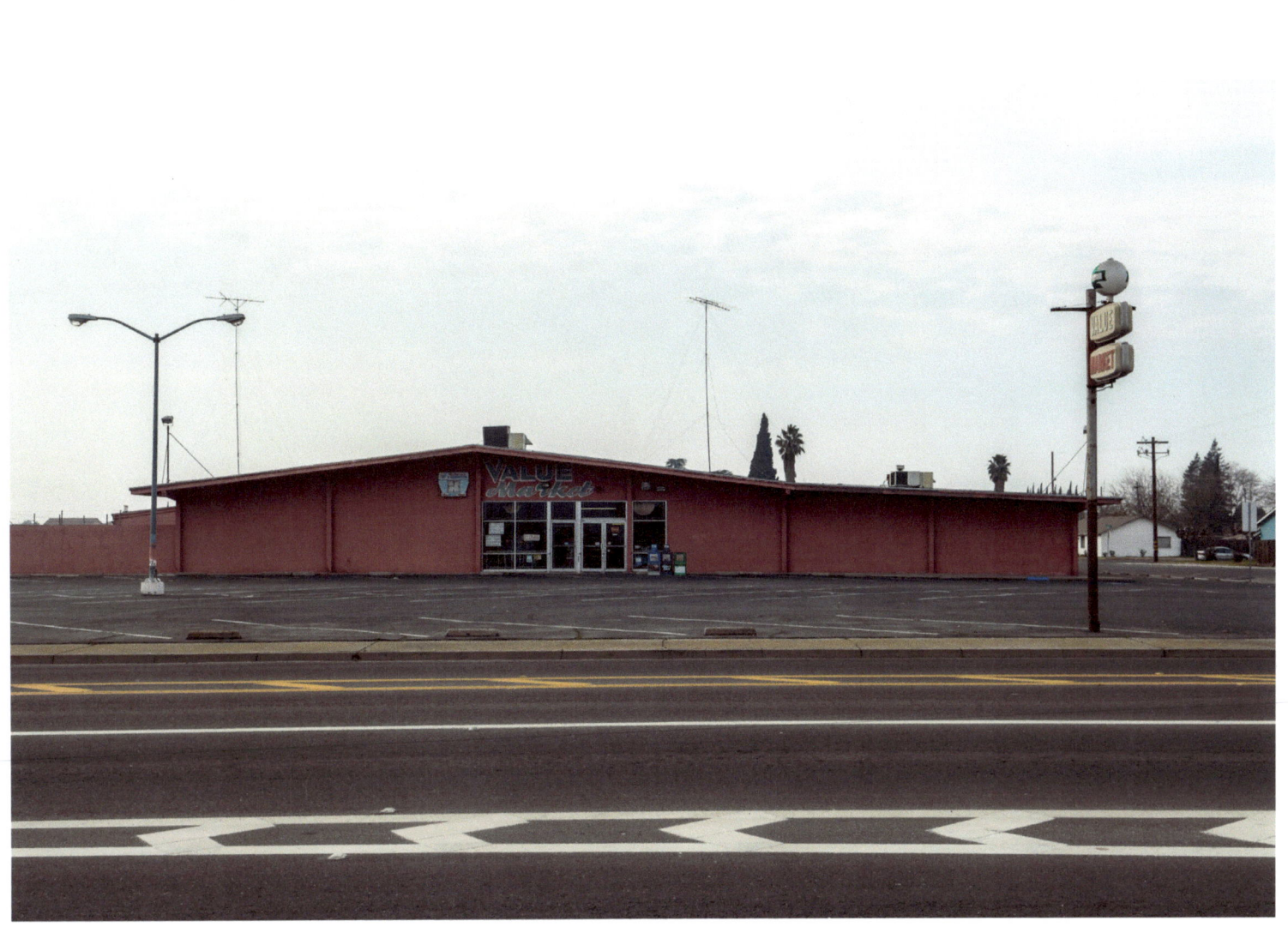

14. Mendota Food Center, 697 Derrick Avenue, Mendota (1967-2012)

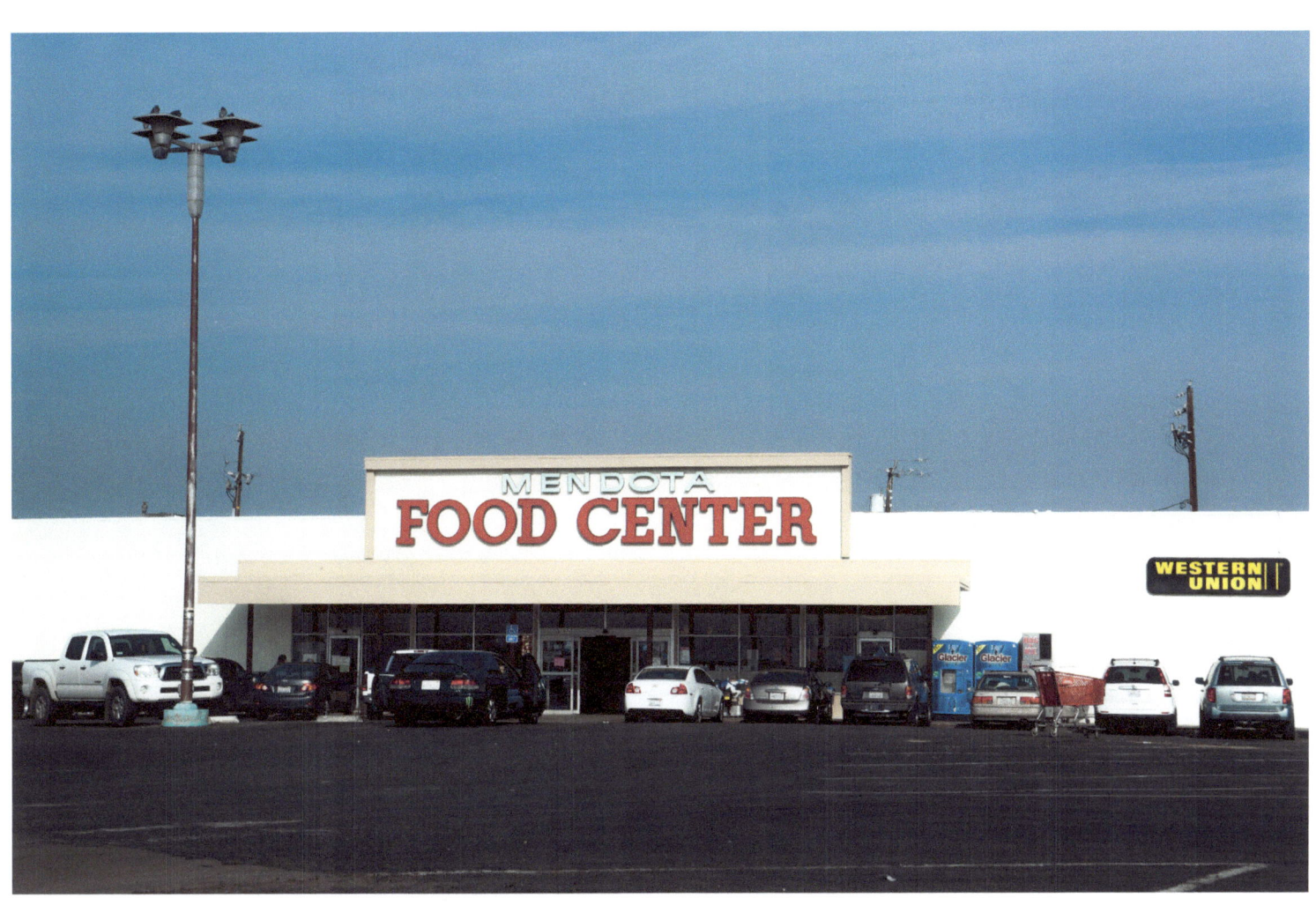

15. Denair Food Center, 4330 Main Street, Denair (1986-2002)

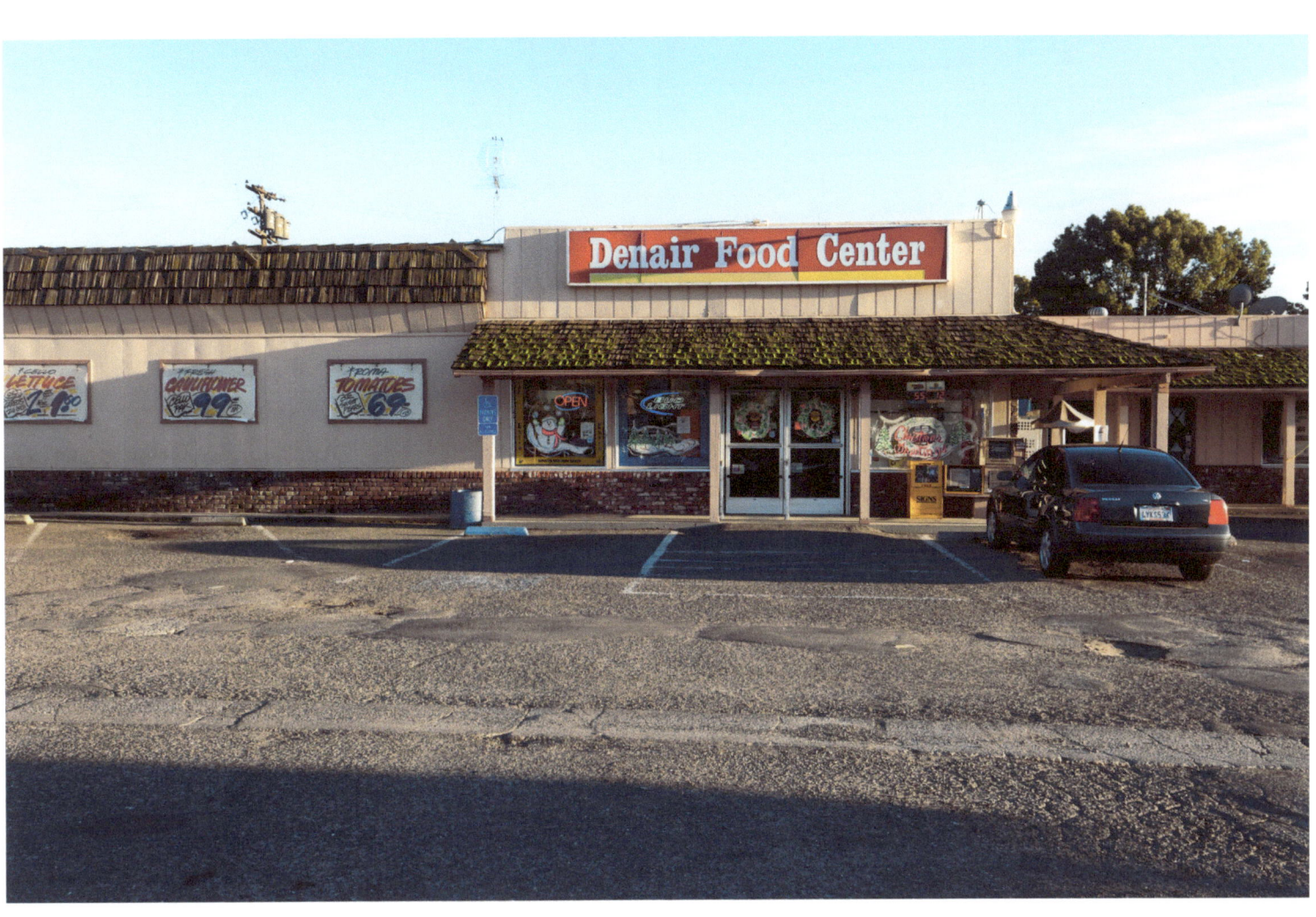

16. Liberty Market, 200 North Second Street, Patterson (1953-2001)

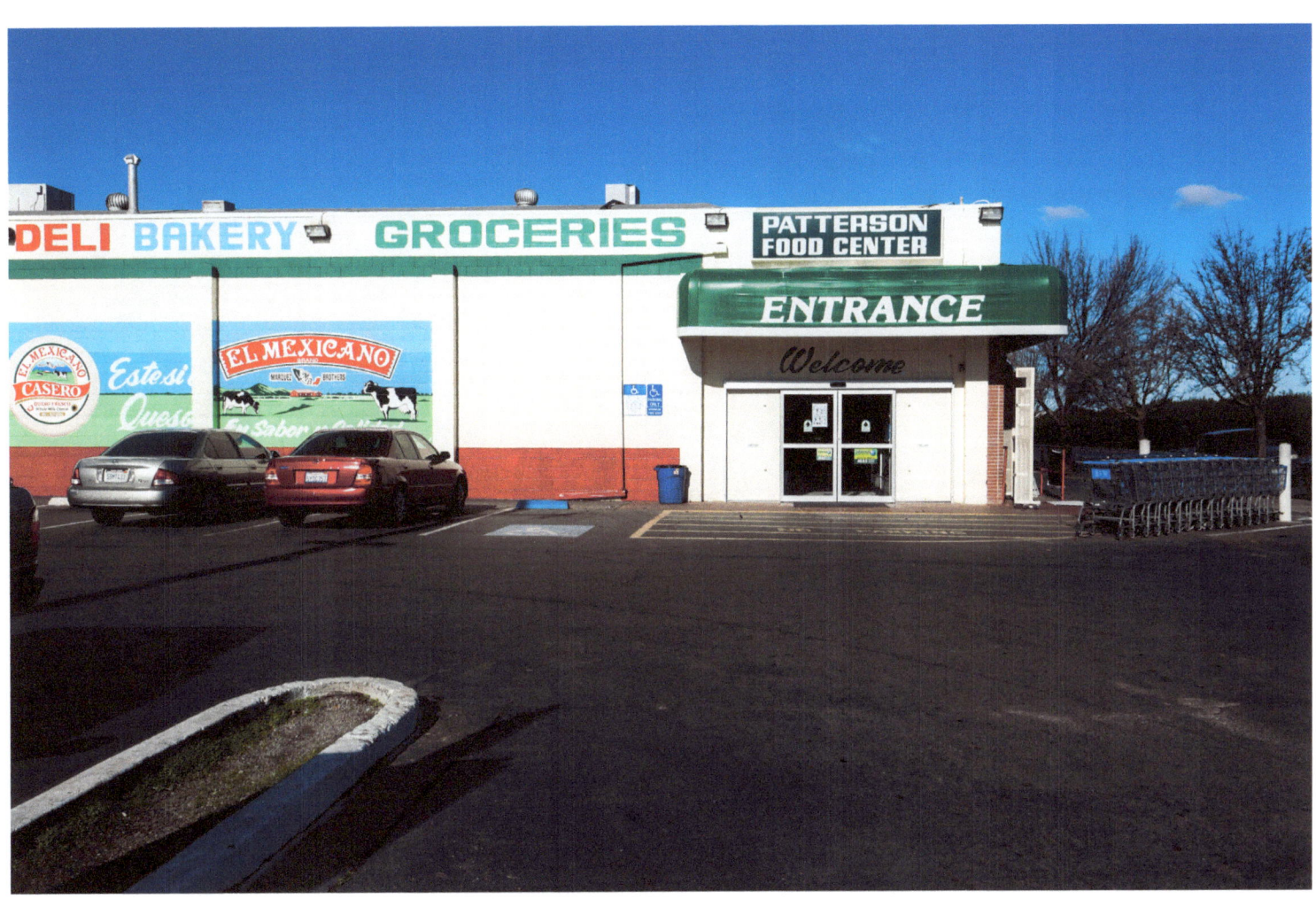

17. Riverbank Food Center, 3501 Atchison Street, Riverbank (1959-c. 1974)

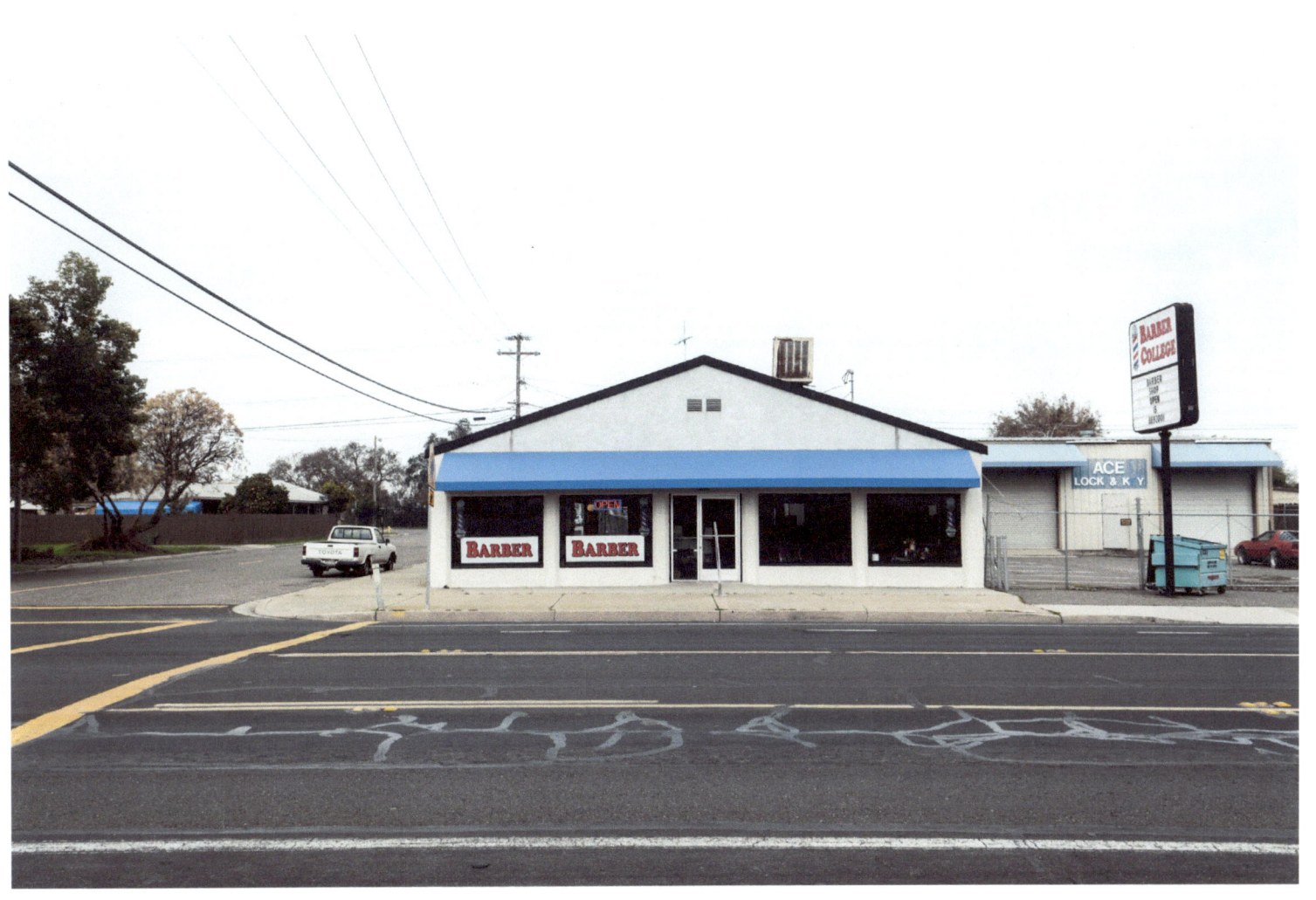

18. Riverbank Food Center II, 6450 Third Street, Riverbank (c. 1974-late 1990s)

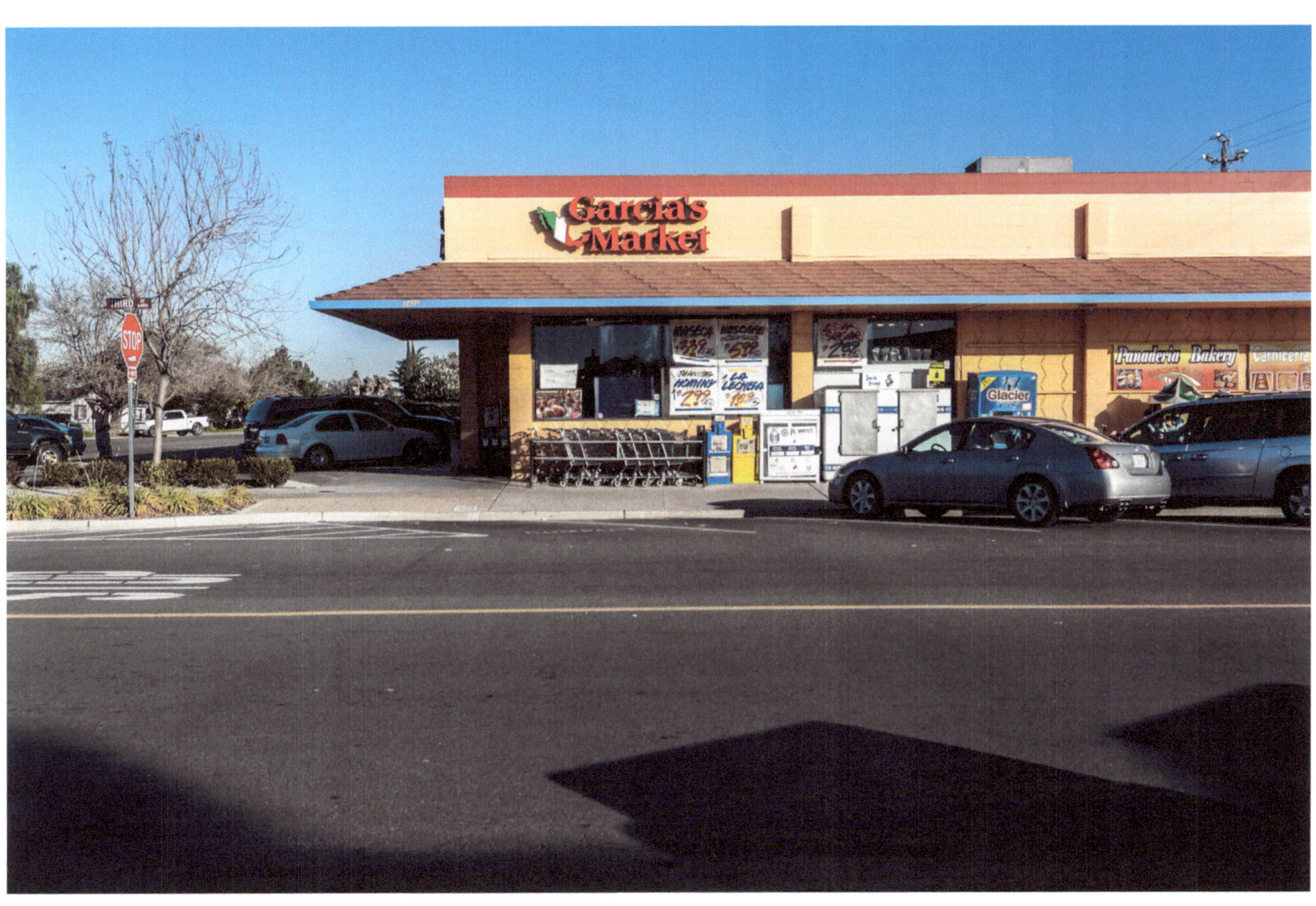

19. Valley Food Center, 12705 Bentley Street, Waterford (1960-1967)

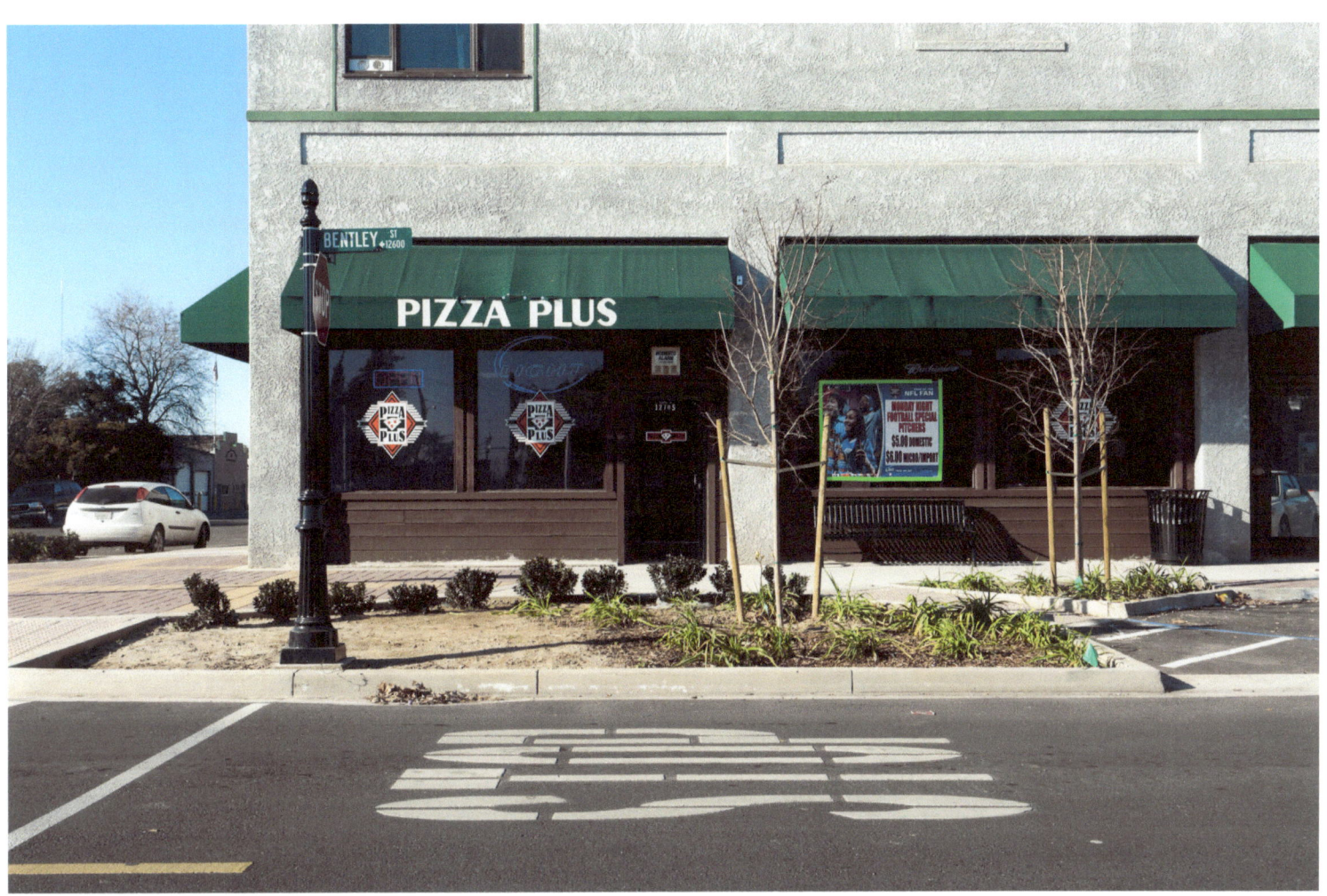

20. Valley IGA, 120 F Street, Waterford (1967-1996)

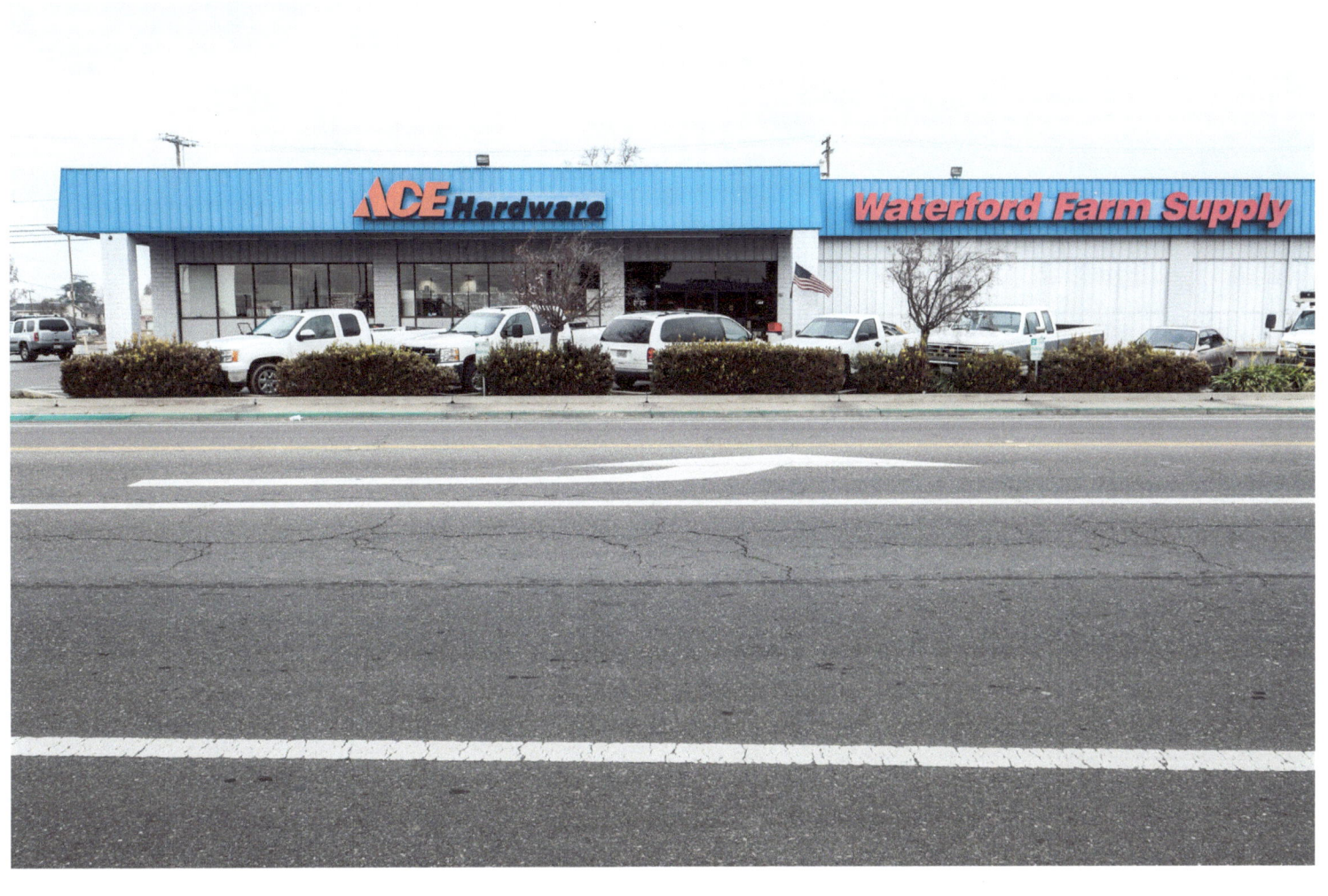

21. Valley IGA II, 12138 Yosemite Boulevard, Waterford (1996-)

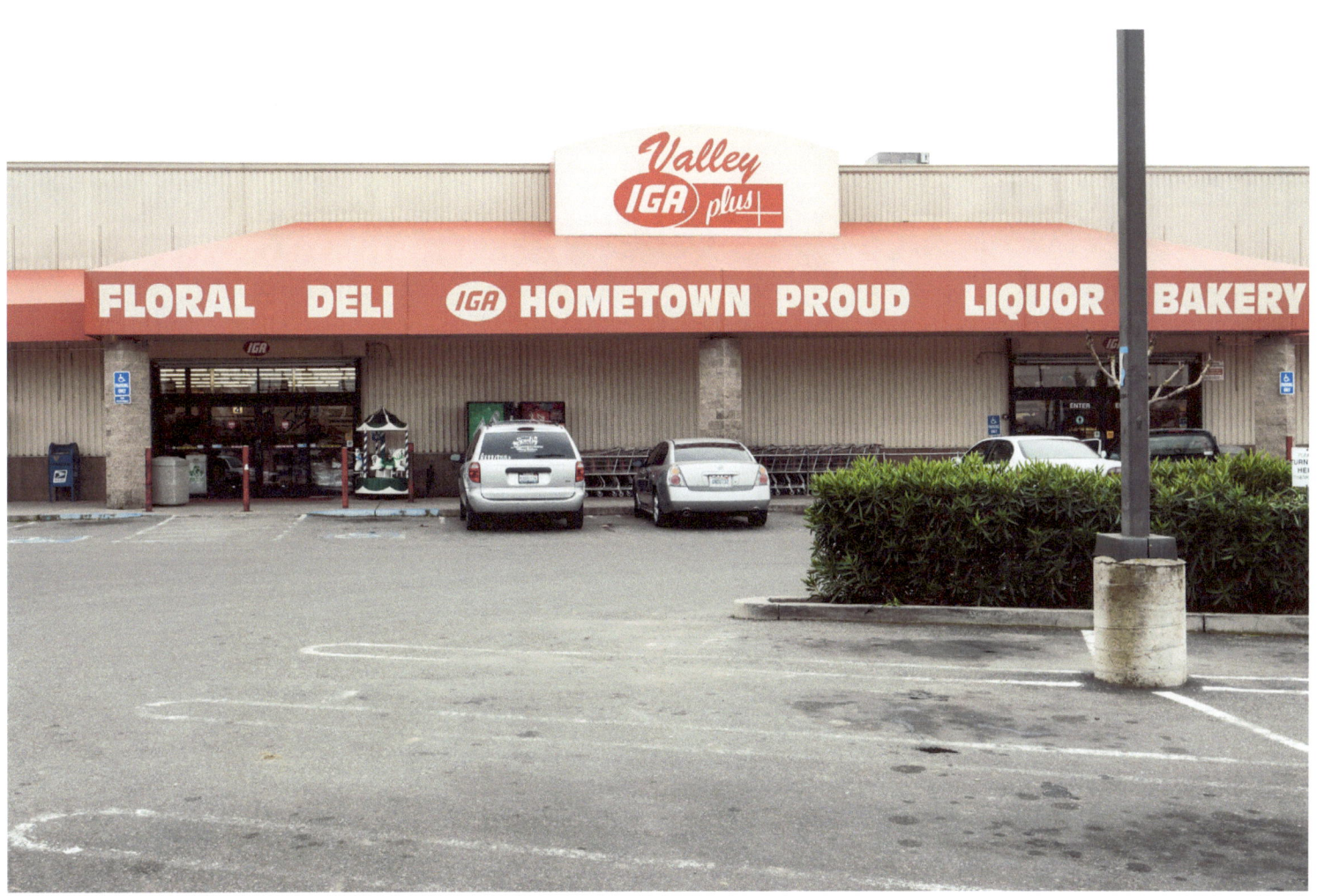

22. Home

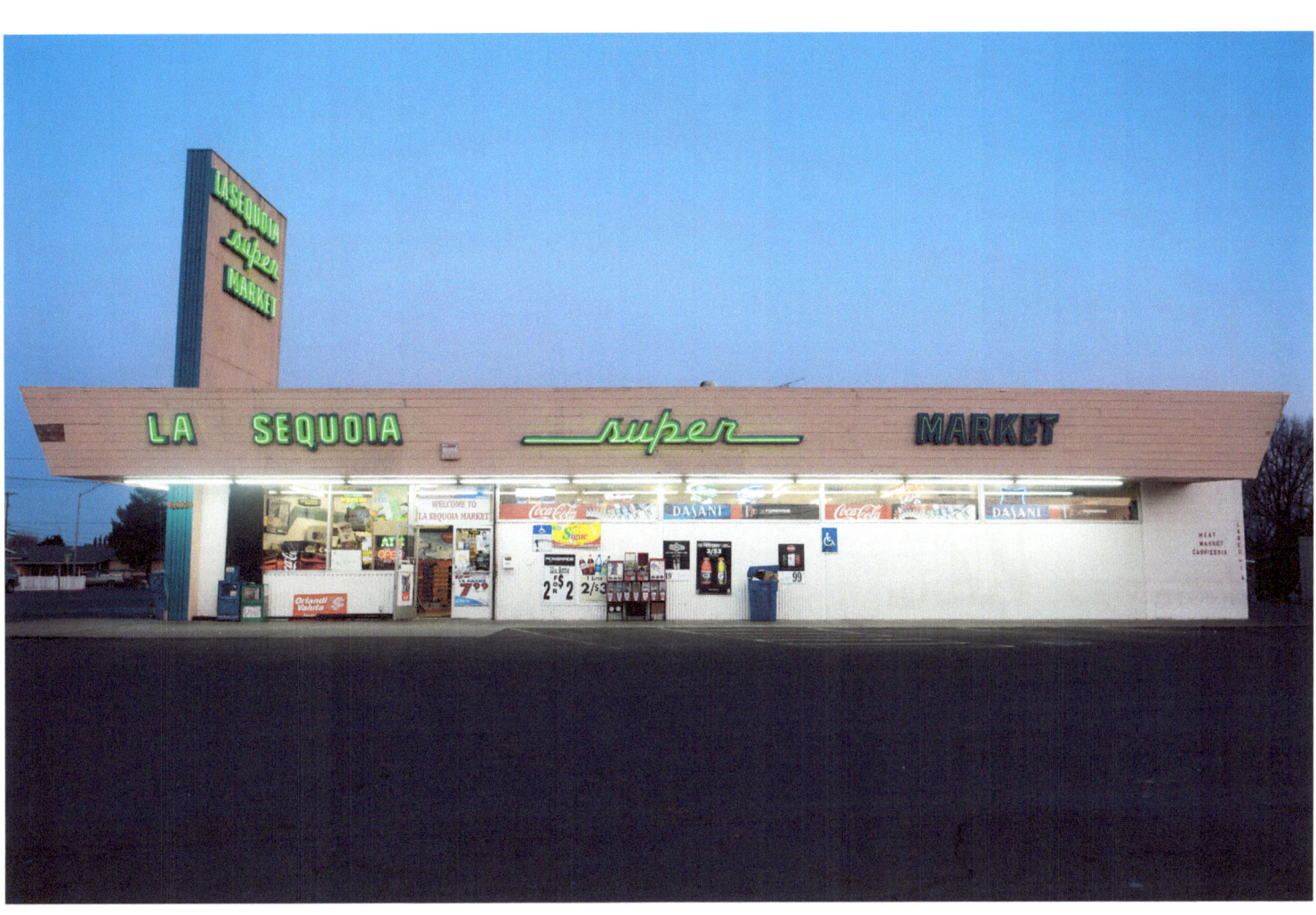

Appendix: List of Stores:

1. Palace Market, 120 North Douty Street, Hanford, (1942-1954)

2. Sequoia Super Market, 2000 North Central Avenue, Ceres (1955-2005)

3. Red and White Market, 445 East F Street, Oakdale (c. 1955-1971)
4. Monte Food Market, 2202 East Fremont Street, Stockton (c. 1972-1985)

5. Sam's Food City I, 1046 Fresno Street, Newman, (1954-1988)
6. Sam's Food City II, 1100 Carver Road, Modesto (1962-2013)
7. Sam's Food City III, 323 Cressey Road, Livingston (1981-2013)
8. Sam's Food City IV, 125 South Circulo Avenue, Patterson (1985-2012)
9. Sam's Food City V, 444 West F Street, Oakdale (1990s)
10. Sam's Food City VI, 965 Lander Avenue, Turlock (1997-2013)

11. National Market, 1290 East Avenue, Turlock (1951-)

12. Livingston Food Center, 334 Main Street, Livingston (mid-1950s-1963)
13. Value Market, 1724 Main Street, Livingston, (1963-)

14. Mendota Food Center, 697 Derrick Avenue, Mendota (1967-2012)

15. Denair Food Center, 4330 Main Street, Denair (1986-2002)

16. Liberty Market, 200 North Second Street, Patterson (1953-2001)

17. Riverbank Food Center, 3501 Atchison Street, Riverbank (1959-c. 1974)
18. Riverbank Food Center II, 6450 Third Street, Riverbank (c. 1974-late 1990s)

19. Valley Food Center, 12705 Bentley Street, Waterford (1960-1967)
20. Valley IGA, 120 F Street, Waterford (1967-1996)
21. Valley IGA II, 12138 Yosemite Boulevard, Waterford (1996-2013)

Artist's Note: Stores in bold denote original stores owned by various family members. Stores listed underneath are descendent of those original stores. All stores closed in 2013 were closed after January 2013, and are thus noted as being extant in the body of the work.

www.ingramcontent.com/pod-product-compliance
Lightning Source LLC
Chambersburg PA
CBHW040747200526
45159CB00023B/1770